MEMOIR AMERICAN

MEMOIR AMERICAN

Benjamin Hollander

dead letter office

BABEL Working Group

punctum books ＊ brooklyn, ny

Memoir American
© Benjamin Hollander, 2013.

http://creativecommons.org/licenses/by-nc-nd/3.0/

This work is Open Access, which means that you are free to copy, distribute, display, and perform the work as long as you clearly attribute the work to the authors, that you do not use this work for commercial gain in any form whatsoever, and that you in no way alter, transform, or build upon the work outside of its normal use in academic scholarship without express permission of the author and the publisher of this volume. For any reuse or distribution, you must make clear to others the license terms of this work.

First published in 2013 by
dead letter office, BABEL Working Group
an imprint of punctum books
Brooklyn, New York
http://punctumbooks.com

The BABEL Working Group is a collective and desiring-assemblage of scholar-gypsies with no leaders or followers, no top and no bottom, and only a middle. BABEL roams and stalks the ruins of the post-historical university as a multiplicity, a pack, looking for other roaming packs and multiplicities with which to cohabit and build temporary shelters for intellectual vagabonds. We also take in strays.

ISBN-13: 978-0615808628
ISBN-10: 061580862X

Cover Image: details from Lucas van Valckenborch, *Tower of Babel* (1594), Louvre Museum.

Table of Contents

Whose Babel	1
Like a Rumor through the Fact of Translation	3
Oscarine and Jacques and Me	7
Like a Rumor	9
Clear, Concise, Correct: A Drama	17
The Eloquence in Question: Reznikoff's "Manner"	21
Brandon Brown and Benjamin Hollander	35
References	55

Acknowledgments

I would like to thank the editors of *A Review of Two Worlds: French and American Poetry in Translation, Sagetrieb* (Spring and Fall, 1992), Charles Reznikoff Issue, and *Bombay Gin* #32, where sections of this manuscript first appeared.

"I take my title from the French word for 'memory' and the American word . . ."

"You take 'American' to sound French, *Américain* . . ."

"I take my title . . ."

"You take it to sound . . ."

"But if memory serves me"

"I am neither French nor American"

(bound)

Memoir American

Benjamin Hollander

§ Whose Babel

You can only be invited to have your say ...

(which I did)

when Guy Bennett and Beatrice Mousli asked me to participate in a conference ...

in 2003, at the University of Southern California, which chronicled the historical and contemporary correspondences between French and American poetry, in translation. I was on a panel with, among others, the translators Pierre Joris and Juliette Valery. To the questions Guy and Beatrice asked us to consider, I first spoke about "Like a Rumor Through The Fact of Translation," as well as to the family story of Oscarine, Jacques Derrida and me, and, later, towards a book which existed like a rumor, for Juliette and Emmanuel and me.

§ Like a Rumor through the Fact of Translation

Guy and Beatrice have asked:

"What is the original text in translation?"

"What is the nature of collaboration in translation?"

"What, exactly, is the relationship between source and target text changing?"

(so, among all these poets and translators, I'll begin with a simple claim)

I am no translator. I am (the) other, the source of someone else's beautiful or miserable translation.

There's little work in being the source of someone else's beautiful or miserable translation, something Walter Benjamin instinctively knew when he refused to call his classic essay "The Task of the Translated."

I don't mind being translated—in fact, I look forward to it in precisely the same way one anticipates returning home. In other words, or in the other's words, being translated is a personal story, sometimes an extension of a family story, as if my poetry might not have a home without it.

Guy and Beatrice have asked: "What is the original text in translation?" But given the story I'm about to tell, I can only ask: What is the original text if not in translation? In other words, for me, how could it exist otherwise but in the other language—first?

This is not an academic story. This is not a "my poetics" story. It's a much more personal story inscribed in my book, *The Book Of Who Are Was,* a collection of poems where characters or figures—like lost and found letters—traverse time, encounter each other, correspond, and appear and disappear, as words do in translation.

As it was written, the book depended on a hope and a question:

How would a future reader be implicated in the theatre of its writing, as if in collaboration with the writer?

Or more to the point: how would the family history I told within it reach this reader, so that the book itself would become a corresponding family history between me and another who found (herself in) it outside the time of its writing.

This (therefore) will have been the story about the nature of collaboration in translation, the family story of Oscarine and Jacques and me.

§ OSCARINE AND JACQUES AND ME

In 1992, I am invited to The Center of Poetry and Translation at *Fondation Royaumont*—a royal medieval abbey turned cultural center 30 miles north of Paris on the Oise River—to have excerpts of my unpublished manuscript, *The Book Of Who Are Was*, translated by a collective of translators. The book begins with a citation from the philosopher Jacques Derrida, which reads in translation: "This (therefore) will not have been a book." Other words of his are embedded in my narrative.

Among the translators at *Royaumont* in 1992 is Oscarine Bosquet, who takes up the task of finishing the translation of the text once I leave the collaborators at *Royaumont*.

Oscarine and I correspond over the years, in which time she marries. In 1997, six months before the book is published in English with Douglas Messerli's Sun & Moon Press, a condensed French version—*Le Livre De Qui Sont Était*—appears under Oscarine's signature. It's certainly not the first time a translation exists as a published book while the original is still forthcoming. Still, I wonder: What—and where —is the original text if not in translation? And how could it exist otherwise but in the second language first?

When the book is issued in English, I send a copy to the philosopher Jacques Derrida, whom I don't know, but who writes me a beautiful note, and I admire it so much that I name it to friends, a letter. I wonder, however: which book is he admiring? He must, I assume, have seen the French edition six months earlier. He must have seen it, I assume, not because he knows who I am as a poet, but because he knows who the translator has become over the years: the translator Oscarine Bosquet who has—yes—married the son of the philosopher Jacques Derrida, whose words, "This (therefore) will not have been a book," are cited in translation in Benjamin Hollander's *The Book Of Who Are Was*, the hope of which depended on how future readers would be implicated in the theatre of its writing, as if in collaboration with its writer. Or, more to the point, on how its writer and its future readers would make of the book itself a corresponding family history outside the time of its writing, as have Oscarine and Jacques, who have written with me: "This (therefore) will not have been a book," never only a book, never only an academic story, but a much more personal story about the nature of collaboration in translation:

How could the book exist otherwise?

§ LIKE A RUMOR

for

Juliette and Emmanuel and me

re: the question,

"What, exactly, is the relationship between source and target text

changing?"

Did I tell you I was born in Israel? Well, I'll get back to it, as one source. In the meantime, let me say:

If I am the source of someone else's translation, how does the translation change me and the poem?

The source of my poem "Ȯnȯme" was sounded in the dark: I turned off the lights, the appliances, double locked the door, drew the curtains, and I started writing without seeing the words before me. After a half hour, I switched on the lights. Letters were spiraling and circling into each other on the page. I saw three syllables over and over, which I pronounced *Ȯnȯme*, almost like an omen: *Ȯnȯme Ȯnȯme Ȯnȯme*. It sounded like a figure on the run, like a rumor. A scare tactic in the dark. It worked. On me.

It worked so well that I lost sight of the three words actually spelled out before me—not "Ȯnȯme," but O No Me, a startling bit of self-recognition, as if the whole time I had sounded "Ȯnȯme," I couldn't know or see the "me" in it, as if the word scared me out of my own skin. Is this what Oppen meant when he said: "When the man writing is frightened by a word, he may have started." I started it—like a rumor.

When Emmanuel Hocquard and Juliette Valéry saw it, their translation and publication of this poem started another rumor, which changed it.

In English, the poem is 2-3 pages. In French, it's almost the same. Yet the rumor I hear suggests its reception among the French, and thus maybe its status, is different, different enough to have changed it in English.

In French, the small poem has appeared as a small book. This is Juliette's chapbook—her *Format Américain* series. But it was only a small poem, only a few pages when I started it.

In French, I hear, it is sometimes taught, the way a book is sometimes taught.

In French, it has appeared in several anthologies of American poets in translation and one time, most curiously, in an anthology of mostly *French* poets. In English, my poetry has not appeared in even one anthology of mostly *American* poets.

In French, it's been critiqued in a review of "detective novels in France," as if it were a book, a novel, long: the reviewer called it "a detective poem," a *"poème policier"*—a genre unto its own, I suppose. Maybe that's why, being a genre of its own in French, no one needs to call it much of anything in English. These are the rumors I hear about its reception in French, in translation, so how does the fact of this translation change my small poem in English? And, if we are charting the here of there, how does its "thereness" in French affect this small poem here in English?

Well, I make it—what else—a book, the book in English it never intended to be. That is, seeing how Emmanuel and Juliette have spread the word of this 2-3-page poem like a rumor through the fact of translation, I write 30 more pages. I follow their lead. And partly because of them, I perpetuate the rumor I started.

"Ȯnȯme" the name becomes a character. It turns into a figure of speech, "Onoma," the contraction of a Greek phrase meaning, "the Being that is avidly sought." On the run. Like a rumor. Like, ah, Bartleby the Scrivener. It lurks under the sign of "anomie," the name for what Emile Durkheim calls urban lawlessness. A figure on the run like a rumor in Durkheim's urban lawlessness, it transforms into the detective poem it never intended to be. In English, it incarnates the atmosphere of the poem the French reviewer said was like experiencing someone "after an evening of drinking, when one is too much seeing things ahead of their representations." As if it's always discovering the name it could be but is not. As in translation: where, Emmanuel says (and I cite it), "language itself can turn to rumour."

And so it does with *Ònòme*, which generates a long companion sequence called "Levinas and the Police"—where another Emmanuel (Levinas) follows like a rumour what the first Emmanuel (Hocquard) started. With me. With Juliette. With Emmanuel, who has written: "To translate American poetry into French is to gain ground," so that the "surface area" "of French literature" "is expanded into unexplored zones. ... Unowned territory. No man's land." "No French poet could ever write this," he says.

Yes, I agree: "No French poet could ever write this." But having been born in Israel and given my particularly accented and ambiguous relation to American English, I have to say about my poetry a fact Emmanuel already knows: that "no American could ever write this." Which, if my poetry is read in translation more hospitably than it is at home, makes for a startling bit of non-self (or nonsense) recognition: that "no French poet could ever write this which no American [poet] could ever write." This No-man's land and this No-One Land: this being in the poetry of the extra-territorial or, to use Giorgio Agamben's phrase, "reciprocal extraterritorialities."

Is this the ideal political poetic imaginary? A curious state to be in which is, curiously, not a state at all but a future condition (*État*), "unowned territory" which is neither French nor American but is negotiated by the rumor of a poetry which emerges from both, or, if I think about the territory where I am really from—the source of my sources—would neither be called Israel nor Palestine but the rumor of a land emerging from both, a future condition (*État*) which seeks the name it could be but is not.

As in translation.

Second American Fact:

"My Motto has always been clear, concise, correct."

~Bob Sheppard, NY Yankees Stadium Announcer

THE BOOK OF WHO ARE WAS

*

Benjamin Hollander

§ Clear, Concise, Correct: A Drama

Actors: B & U

B: Hi, I'm calling because I'm interested in finding out if you, that is, whether you, have a certain book in stock.

U: Certainly, let me log (you) in.

B: Thank you.

U: Can you give me the title?

B: Yes. (slowly enunciating each word) *The Book Of Who Are Was*, by Benjamin Hollander.

U: (heard typing) *The Book of* ... I'm sorry—could you repeat that?

B: Certainly: *The Book Of Who Are Was*, by Benjamin Hollander.

U: O.K.—let me type it in ... *The Book of Who I Was*?

B: No, I'm sorry—it's "*are was.*"

U: It's what?

B: Benjamin Hollander's *The Book Of Who Are Was.*

U: *The Book Of Who Benjamin Hollander Was?*

B: No, he's the author.

U: Who?

B: Hollander

U: Of What?

B: *The Book of Who Are—A.R.E.—Was.*

U: Oh, *The Book of Who You Were.* Is that it? (silence on the line) Are you still there?

B: Yes, I'm still here

U: Is it *The Book Of Who You Were?*

B: It is not.

U: It is not? Are you certain?

B: (reading Kamau Brathwaite over the phone)

> it is not
> it is not
> it is not enough
> it is not enough to be free
>   of the red white and blue
>
> it is not
> it is not
> it is not enough
> to be pause, to be hole
> to be void, to be silent
> to be semicolon, to be semicolony

So Brathwaite says in "History of the Voice": "What I am going to talk about this morning is language from the Caribbean, the process of using English in a different way from the 'norm.' English in a new sense as I prefer to call it. English in an ancient sense. English in a very traditional sense. And sometimes not English at all, but language."

So I wonder, in like-minded correspondence: where a book is somewhat unpronounceable in English, as if the original already existed in a vocabulary and syntax alien to native speakers of English, as if it were not at home in its own skin, as if it were already in translation, summoned, as it were, to what could be called The House on un-American Poetry, would it be any more sayable to an American bookseller if he were being asked to look for, say, *Le Livre De Qui Sont Était?*"

Or would its eloquence be in question?

§ THE ELOQUENCE IN QUESTION: REZNIKOFF'S "MANNER"

A few weeks ago, rereading Charles Reznikoff, I thought to write a piece on the fifteenth poem in the second section of *By The Manner (sic) Of Living And Seeing* [see full text of poem in Appendix to this section of the essay]. Out of "The Eloquence of Question," and "The Eloquence at Question," the above title was chosen as the one which sounded "most correct" for a piece still un-written. Why did the eloquence of how to say this elude me? I knew that to choose one title and suppress the others would be to tell a story about how one manner of English gets written under the influence of what does not see print. Fumbling in the head for the correct preposition, I would force the title to manifest a fluency in standard English ("The Eloquence *in* Question"), which masked a failure of what is not ("The Eloquence of Question").

Unlike the other Objectivists, Reznikoff is not a poet I have spent much time reading. Perhaps I have avoided him because I have become too dependent on how others *see* him.

The emphasis is almost always with certainty on the poet's eye. The focus is on focus. The critical literature is a naming of Reznikoff the legal visualist, the neutral observer of working class and cityscape, the arhetorical, underrated, prophet's eye removing the "I" from the scene, the *precisionary* witness excising contemporary from historic particulars, the man of other men's and women's testimony showing itself without his judgment through the clear lines of his poetry. All these readings suggest Reznikoff's confidence in the act of seeing and in the use of an English that would represent it. Few confidently question that confidence, that focus, that use of English. In fact, when the focus is not on the poet's eye, it is on his ability to know and invoke American speech well enough to capture its essential rhythms and sounds. There is a decisiveness to that last proposition, and I'm not sure about it.

What strikes me about this fifteenth poem, and the others across this section of the book, is the indecision and questionable fluency of the poet's voice. Is it or is it not standard American English? What is standard American English in it and what is accented by an "alien" inflection. *Furthermore, how is an American poet's voice transformed when it is written under the influence of other languages which do not need to manifestly show themselves to be "felt present" in the poem, and which we know are evidenced in the poet's life?* What of what he hears in another language—Reznikoff, we know, heard and spoke Yiddish as a child—gets "translated" into his misrepresentations of English, whether intentionally or not? And what of what he hears of misspoken English—Reznikoff's mother had a very limited knowledge of English—gets "translated" into his (mis)representations of the poem's language? Obviously, this is nearly impossible to pin down and detect precisely in terms of causal links, but this is not to ignore the effects of a manner of intonation in some of Reznikoff's work that may suggest some strange and estranged turns in his use of language which this poem, in particular, highlights.

The poem enacts a common enough scene. The speaker witnesses two (most likely) immigrants sitting on a (most likely) NYC bus and speaking in what we assume is their (most likely) native language (either Greek or Italian—the poet can't decide). A hearing woman, seated, can't stand hearing it. The speaker projects a hypothetical clichéd argument, imagining that these immigrants could just as easily be Jews who, if they knew "enough English," would shut the woman up by claiming their status as free citizens able to speak any language they wanted in "a free country" (either that "or they might become silent"). The woman, however, will not shut up, and she wants comforting. She jumps up, sits next to the speaker, and asks his opinion about these crazy foreigners unable to speak the native lingo. Carefully, the speaker rationalizes the men's condition and behavior as immigrants. The woman looks "suspiciously" at the speaker and rushes off the bus, as if she knows (or hears) he is one of "them." Finally, the men, "in the best of American," fluent in a language they have concealed from the woman, quietly say to the speaker: "She's a little cracked, isn't she?"

On one level, this poem addresses typical xenophobic assumptions, where the ability to speak in the common tongue tests an immigrant's worth and place in American society, and becomes a prerequisite for "free citizenry" among "English Only" Americans. Given the opportunity to "make their money here," the foreigners' debt to the country should be repaid in full in the linguistic currency of their adopted home. Anything less is a sign of arrogance and ingratitude.

The narrator, of course, is familiar with this attitude, and so are the two men, whose refusal to speak the language is not from lack of knowledge but from a resistance to the woman's demands. They can distinguish all too well when and for whom private understanding of a language should be publicly acknowledged or withheld. The narrator also knows this, but is willing to—perhaps he can't not—reveal his "accent" in English, as is shown in the woman's reaction to him. But what kind of "accent" is this? How can we tell? Does the narrator know it himself? Is it Reznikoff's? The answers depend on the paradoxical locutions and word choices in the poem.

> Two men were seated near me in a bus;
> well dressed, well-fed; in the forties;

The first two lines frame a perfect description in English, except the two men are "in the forties." It's strange to hear this as an era, but not so strange to hear it as a (common ESL) mistake, where the more appropriate "in *their* forties" would be expected. One might also expect the colon after "bus" to yield three specific modifiers for the men, certainly not a generalized time frame. This is not an isolated example of Reznikoff's "the"-for-"their" switch, which appears elsewhere in this part of the book. If we assume Reznikoff is the speaker, then it seems as if he is also formalizing his accent, eloquently distancing from the foreigners yet overcompensating a bit—sounding himself a touch foreign in the process. As such, it is "the"-not-"their speech" we hear. Curiously, however, and perhaps purposefully, Reznikoff's eloquence is not consistent, since he chooses the colloquial "talk" to represent how "men of good breeding and education" might, ideally, "speak." Is Reznikoff confused or is he just playing with our preconceptions about good English? I am unsure, yet I sense he is doing both, particularly when the question of what

English is in question.

When the woman, for instance, says, "Why don't they talk American?" she may be talking like some Americans but not like someone from NYC, who would most likely say, "Why don't they speak English?" One of three things could be happening here: First, Reznikoff could be correctly citing the woman, in which case we have someone whose language ("talk American") assumes a down-home antagonism grounded in mis-projected class differences she discerns between herself and "men of good breeding and education," intellectuals who she senses (even as she does not understand them) are not of her class (odd that she doesn't notice that they, like her, are also riding the bus). Second, Reznikoff could be drawing distinctions between American and English—as the French translate from the American, not English—thus showing his sensitivity to the differences between the two, a particularly ironic awareness, given his "accent" across the poem. Finally, he could be somewhat blind to the differences, in which case he really believes he knows English—at least his brand, perhaps learned abroad or influenced by those who have come from abroad—and is not familiar with the American version. As a Jew, he imagines a scenario where other Jews, isolated in the same context, perhaps like himself, would turn to the woman and uneasily say, "This is a free country, isn't it?" If, that is, they "knew enough English," not "American." Reznikoff may be projecting himself as one of those Jews, whose English is always learned "abroad" and accented, however slightly, no matter how fluent. Yes, "English is not an easy language to learn," since no matter how well educated and well-bred one is, it is, after all, recognized as English and not American, never echoing smoothly within a certain class of American speech and society.

If we listen to Reznikoff's language, it is not difficult to detect its foreign tenor. First, there is his insistence on English—not American—which he, the men, and the imaginary Jews might be speaking here. Second, in the best of formal, eloquent English—sounding a bit like the well-meaning lecturer—and without a note of urban contentiousness, he reasons:

> You must not be so impatient ...
> English is not an easy language to learn.
> Besides, if they don't learn it, their children will:
> We have good schools, you know.

The "there, there, my dear" *manner of intonation*—as well as the request for understanding—is why the woman looks at him "suspiciously" and why she flees the foreign "contamination" which Reznikoff, in saying "our contamination," now confesses he exudes. But it is the last few lines that suggest what this woman senses, which is Reznikoff's position among these "other" men. It is not only that "the best of American" is an odd turn on "the best of English" (perhaps Reznikoff—as outsider—does not know the right way of putting it), but that the phrase, "She's a little cracked, isn't she," does not sound American or urban American in its register of bemused reticence. Even if one could argue—and I think one could—that there is nothing un-American about this expression, it seems strange to me that Reznikoff, who has already marked his "accent" in other ways across this poem, would know it (or know it to be "the best of *American*"). Perhaps my dilemma about whether this expression is American or not is exactly the point, since its ambiguity puts Reznikoff's relation to the language (American or English) and the men in question. His "accent," as such, is undetermined, provisional and fluid, depending on context. He can mimic the (possibly) American expression, at the same time as he can create doubt about its and his authenticity within the American language and culture: seemingly invisible—he is, perhaps, the most dangerous kind of their kind.

To identify Reznikoff with the speaker and these men is not to deny his distance from them. In other words, his knowledge of American and English could be extensive and confident enough that he is playfully and ironically creating this scene outside of himself. My guess, however, is that the irony has been *composed* after the fact—perhaps as the poem was revised—and that it does not preclude the accidents of poor standard American English (as well as the confusion between American and English) which initially surface in the writing of the poem. Or it could be that irony and literality are simultaneously exposed here, where the mis-locutions are initially unwilled and then immediately realized, giving Reznikoff the chance to play with his mistakes for the sake of the reader (fluently covering his "foreign" tracks, so to speak).

If we turn to what Reznikoff said about his relationship to language(s), we see that the distinctions—whether he could make them or not—between American and English were not lost on him. In a 1974 interview with Reinhold Schiffer (*Charles Reznikoff: Man and Poet*, National Poetry Foundation, 1984), Reznikoff admits that, "American common speech, well, it hasn't got to me, it hasn't got, say, the music that Irish speech has, and English, but I try to supply it." Unlike William Carlos Williams, who notes in his translation of Sappho that, "I don't speak English, but the American idiom. I don't know how to write anything else, and I refuse to learn," Charles Reznikoff, as if he were in conversation with Carlos Williams, counters: " I don't find anything in *American* speech as such, but of course my medium is English. My medium is English, not that I chose it, but, let me say [laughs], God chose it for me, and that's the speech I know, somewhat." Obviously, Reznikoff's "somewhat" could be taken as a simple, tongue-in-cheek tag. I suspect, however, that it could also indicate his lack of confidence and full trust in the English medium, with that word "medium" representing a site not chosen, unowned, perhaps, in some way, outside of Reznikoff's being, even as a native-born American poet writing in what looks like English as a first language. It may not be that Reznikoff felt isolated in English (which he claimed he did not in another interview), but only that he recognized it as a medium he used outside the place he lived and practiced his poetry. It may certainly be, however, that he felt isolated in *American*, no matter how well he might be able to mimic, in his work, what he heard of this talk.[1]

What I hear, then, in Reznikoff's "manner," is a poem guided by errors in fluency which are evidence of the traces of the language which is not American, influenced by and "translated" from an

---

[1] Many years later, as I was walking up the stairs dwelling on what Carlos Williams had said, that he "don't speak English, but the American idiom. I don't know how to write anything else, and I refuse to learn," I remembered an old friend of Charles, Carl, who was convinced when I visited with him that my speculation about Reznikoff's so-called un-American American talk was, well, a bit ambiguous, a bit cracked and intellectual. It didn't walk the speech Carl heard from Charles: "Why don't you talk American?" I heard him say, or so I thought, to me, "cause that don't sound like Rezi, to me."

English which tends to sound "a trace of a foreign accent," even as that accent can't be determined. I can hear this crossing between American and English as an act of translation, where, in Myung Mi Kim's words, "a sense of disarticulation (which might in this case be Reznikoff's first impulses appearing as convoluted mistakes in standard American, perhaps informed or misinformed by his living under the conditions of a second language household) comes to an *approximate* articulation" and fluency in English. And I can think of this as the place where speech enters and intones the writing: an awkwardness or strangeness or inarticulateness which might be recognized even as it can't be helped, and which, like "The Eloquence of Question," "is a little cracked."

APPENDIX

Charles Reznikoff, *By The Well of Living and Seeing*, Section 15:

Two men were seated near me in a bus:
well dressed, well-fed; in the forties;
obviously respected members of their community;
talking together calmly,
the way men of good breeding and education talk,
and the speech may have been Greek or Italian.
I could not hear enough of it to decide.
Suddenly a woman seated directly behind them
Began in a loud voice:
"Why don't you talk American?
You live here, don't you?
You make your living here?
Talk American!"

One of the men turned to glance at her
and then the two went on talking in Greek or Italian,
calmly, quietly,
although every now and then the woman cried out,
"Talk American, why don't you?"

If these men were Jews, I thought,
how uneasy they would have become,
and their faces would show it.
One of them might even say to the woman—
if he knew enough English,
"This is a free country, isn't it?"
And there would be a noisy argument.
Or they might become silent.

The two men, however, continued to talk,
as they had been doing,
and neither turned to glance at the woman
or show by gesture or grimace
that they heard her.
Finally, she jumped up and sat down beside me.
"What do you think of these men?" she asked.
"Why don't they talk American?
They live here, don't they?
They make their money here!"

"You must not be so impatient," I said.
"English is not an easy language to learn.
Besides, if they don't learn it, their children will:
we have good schools, you know."
She looked at me suspiciously
and, when the bus stopped, hurried off—
fleeing our contamination.
One of the men then turned to me and said quietly
in the best of American with not a trace of a foreign accent:
"She's a little cracked, isn't she?"

§ Brandon Brown and Benjamin Hollander

NOTE: Between 2004 and 2005, and upon his translation into American English of Horace's Latin *Odes*, Brandon Brown wrote to Benjamin Hollander, who wrote back. This is their correspondence, one from Brown, one from Hollander, both

> about the transference of power through translation, about odes which make emperors and chancellors kneel, about how to return home to disclose "the imprint of the invaded in the language of the master." Which means, in effect, to come home to spy on "your own" as if you yourself were there to be revealed in something that needed to be said about the country, something found in an unsealed memoir, a *Memoir American*.

This correspondence acted without title, once.

If these letters had a title today, they would not stand more revealed …

December 6, 2004

Dear Ben,

Traduttore, tradittore. Translator, traitor. The adage depends on the substitution of the vowel 'i' for 'u' (I for You); its Latin equivalent would depend on the substitution of consonants, the difference between transLation and transDation. Translation: the bearing, carrying across (I prefer "lug across" on one hand because it emphasizes the human body in between writings and on the other displays the pain the body suffers in translating.) Transdation: the handing-over of one. At the very root of any notion of traitorship (tradership) is this handing-over. The adage is equational. The equation in the adage depends on the English words "across" and "over" being not only similar in signification but synonymous. But of course the difference between "make it across the pool" and "hand it over, pal" is precisely the difference the adage puns on, making the equation.

But what kind of traitorship is it? In the Benedict Arnoldian sense, the translator betrays her country by handing-over the precious cultural commodity of the country. Country's wrong. Not country (*pater*) but no less than the mother tongue (*mater*) is handed over. In this sense the translator is a spy, loose-lipped, spilling the secrets before the torture even begins. Do we suppose in our daily practices, writing poetry, that we are acting in secret (dealing in secrets)? The Benedict Arnolds among translators are, of course, the persons who translate the works of their mOther tongue into an Other tongue. What is the traitorship of the translator who translates work from the Other tongue into the mOther tongue? Antoine Berman writes:

> Every culture resists translation, even if it has an essential need for it. The very aim of translation—to open up in writing a certain relation with the Other, to fertilize what is one's Own through the mediation of what is Foreign—is diametrically opposed to the ethnocentric structure of every culture, that species of narcissism by which every society wants to be a pure and unadulterated Whole. There is a tinge of the violence of crossbreeding in translation.

The translator is a traitor in that she hands over the safety of the mother tongue. I desire to betray my mother tongue. Unlike Judas Iscariot, I will not be paid talents of silver for my efforts.

Nor will I have protection. The translator like any spy is at risk.

Love, BB

December 2004 – April 2005

Dear Brandon,

You send me an email and call it a letter, but the letter as "real" mail is never sent. Instead, as the computer jingle goes, "you've got mail," though I really don't (like a dead letter). Though I get it.

You betray your intention. You don't mean to call something that which it is not. You don't mean to call the email you sent me a letter, a dead letter, but you do. You're probably unaware that you're betraying your intention. But you do, and I get it, so you're on to something. Let me tell you: you're on to something. I mean it. Though you might know it.

Let me ask you: how useful is this discussion about translation to how you and I, I and you, see our place in this world in relation to others? That's the question. That's the only question.

Do you really intend to call yourself a traitor? I ask because, for me, it's not a question of literary translation, really. If you call yourself a traitor, you better mean it. You better know what you mean. I mean it. Do you mean it?

* * *

Certainly, you can't mean ALL translators when you write that, "The Benedict Arnolds among translators are, of course, the persons who translate the works of their mOther tongue into an Other tongue." Because what happens, I ask you, when translation is meant as a gift and not as a betrayal?

For example, let's say I offer to translate your poetry into Latin at the request of a Latin scholar curious about why the anti-imperial poet Brandon Brown has undertaken of all things a translation of Horace usually reserved for Latin scholars—a Horace for whom Brandon Brown has "the paradoxical feeling of awe at his metrical capability and skill, and disgust at his war-loving, emperor-revering politics." In translating you, then, am I a "Benedict Arnold among translators" because I have taken the ("our") mOther tongue (English) used by you and have offered it up to the Latinists? It depends, of course, on my intention: on whether my translation bears your poetry as a gift or betrays it like the horse of a gift. It depends, of course, on one's notion of translation.

Certainly, one conventional notion of translation is one that your letter upsets. When one says that an act of betrayal is embedded in the act of translation, one usually means the translator thinks she is a traitor to the intention and the singularity of the poem in the other language, its original language, let's say. That's the conventional lament—

a lament

>   the one
>
>   you upset.

Instead, you write about "Transdation [as] the handing-over of one," about the translator betraying the language she was born into, the language she translates other languages into, her own.

Let me say what you may already know: the hand you're handing over is your own.

Isn't it painful to hand one's own hand over? Isn't that the point? That's the question, the only question.

It may feel like you're doing translation. It may feel like we're in dialogue about it. It may feel this way in the same way it may feel that you think you are a traitor—although these feelings may only be excuses or mediums for handing something of yourself over—on your own.

The question is: what are you really handing over? And what, in the handing over, do you withhold?

Let's say: any language, like any person, has its baggage—what we carry, what we lug, what we keep in confidence, perhaps.

And let's say: any translator when he translates has to deal with the baggage of his mother tongue, with what he thinks he knows best because he's lived so long with(in) it.

The question is: how does he deal with his baggage when he is facing another's? No doubt:

he needs to make room for it, but he can't just accommodate it.

No doubt: bad translation would be good accommodation.

Instead, to deal with his own he must figure out how it relates to the other's unlike(ly) baggage, which is not only not an intrusion but which he willingly hosts, welcomes, so much so that he risks the other (hypothetically) saying, "get out" or "so long" or "make room for me" or "don't make room for me" or "I don't care, just leave and include me at the same time. Turn your baggage inside out, if you have to. Don't just accommodate me."

In reality, (t)his risk is imaginary. The other makes no such demands, but that doesn't mean that the good host doesn't feel compelled to make them for the other. This profound compulsion is what threatens "that species of narcissism by which every society wants to be a pure and unadulterated Whole." It comes from within that society. It comes from within and turns the one who hosts it inside out. The irony, of course, is that a society can only become Whole (though certainly not Pure) when this compulsion precisely and exclusively threatens its "narcissism."

To act on this compulsion is one of the tasks of the translator, as it is for the Israeli publisher and translator Yael Lehrer, whose imprint, Al-Andalus, translates Arabic Literature into Hebrew. To your question, "What is the traitorship of the translator who translates work from the Other tongue into the mOther tongue?" Lehrer might respond: risky but not risky enough, to say the least, because when you are compelled to say the most about your country's "barbarous Arab policy," to translate from the other tongue to the mother tongue is the smallest such sign of cultural protest, still a still small (but only a still small) sign, which can in no way normalize the abnormal relations between occupier and occupied, although it can, one hopes, threaten and eat at the self-image of a society blind "to the crimes that are being perpetrated in [its] name." "Before Israeli readers get to know Arabic literature," Lehrer writes, "they should know AND CARE about the crimes that are being perpetrated in their name. At times like these, it seems that to do anything other than struggle against the occupation is to normalize an unbearable situation. By normalize, I mean treat the abnormal, the intolerable, as if it were routine."

The question is, Brandon, if we are writing about translation (and, as I said before, I'm not sure we are), how can one use translation so that it does not "normalize" relations; that is, so that it does not—will not—easily bear and tolerate an "unbearable situation?" For you, this means subverting the mastery of form in Horace's poems, which are composed in the service of the "war-loving." For Lehrer, it means dealing with her mother tongue, Hebrew, in relation to the people of the "other" tongue, Arabic:

> I was born into this conflict, it wasn't a matter of choice. I was also born into the Hebrew language, my mother tongue as well as that of both my parents. Since I became a conscious adult, I have found this reality intolerable, but more importantly, I have tried to assume responsibility for it. I am the expeller, the dispossessor, the oppressor, the occupier. It was I who riddled the tender 13-year-old body of Iman al-Hams of Rafah with 20 live bullets; it is I who holds the key to the locked gate in the wall that separates Palestinian schoolchildren from their school. Yet in any other country, and any other tongue, I would feel myself a stranger, an immigrant. My fierce criticism of Zionism notwithstanding, it created me, along with several million other native Hebrew speakers whose only homeland was established upon the ruins of another. Knowing this, it is my responsibility to fight for national and civic equality between Arabs and Jews; to work for historic reconciliation based on the Israeli recognition of the Palestinian Right of Return; for a life of partnership, justice, and equality.

To work for "historic reconciliation," Israelis must be integrated into a land they now separate with a wall. They must see themselves as part of the Middle East, and this means, in part, as Arab-Jews. Lehrer cites the Israeli historian Amnon Raz-Krakotzkin:

> The category Arab-Jew isn't merely marking an identity that was and still is the basis for the consciousness of Arab Jews [i.e., Jews who originated in Arab lands]: it is meant to constitute a basis for defining the consciousness of every Israeli, the new basis for Israeli identity, whose existence and right to do so, must be premised on their existence in the Arab world. As long as Israeli discourse is premised on the dichotomy Arab vs. Jew, it will be impossible to frame an alternative. Arab-Jew is, thus, a call for partnership based on the decolonization of Jewish identity in all senses and contexts.

Imagine, then, translation as only one such context—perhaps even a model—for decolonizing one's identity. To take Lehrer's example, this would require us "to imbed Arabic literature into the Hebrew experience; to create a textual middle-ground, an intermediate cultural space that blurs borders but avoids the pitfalls of Orientalism, which distances rather than draws closer. Blurring borders means resisting the hegemonic dictate to separate and refusing to accept the false binary Arab vs. Jew."

Of course, to resist separation is to insist on integrating into one's worldview a history outside the history one knows. It is to divest oneself of one's old narrative interests. It's clear that most Israelis like most anyone else would find this difficult, and they would reflexively reject Lehrer's "fight for historic reconciliation." They would see her kind of "reconciliation" as a betrayal of the national narrative—i.e. our interests—since they would believe that it is not up to US to reconcile with THEM but the other way around. And, curiously and ironically, perhaps they would be right. Perhaps it takes what some would perceive as "betraying one's own" (story, language, belief, people etc.) to reconcile with what one perceives as "the other than one's own" (story, language, belief, people). "To fertilize what is one's Own through the mediation of what is Foreign," as [Antoine] Berman writes, might first mean to let go of what one privileges as one's own in order to allow what is Foreign to cross. That "textual middle ground," that "intermediate cultural space," may only be able to come into being when one dissolves one's own borders, which may (but does not necessarily) depend upon a betrayal of the space one inhabits, of "what is mine."

Have not translators who translate work "from the Other tongue into the mOther tongue" always considered this question of: "what is mine, here, what is yours?" And, Brandon, if you think you are betraying the safety of the mother tongue—of "what is mine, here"—one would have to ask: why would you want to do this? And what do you think is safe about it? Might it be worth naming and describing what is safe about a mother tongue? Might it be worth naming and describing what it would mean to betray that safety as well as how and why one—you—would do this?

For myself, not being like you the one invested in the practice of translation, and with the freedom to speak irresponsibly about these things as a poet who only has a feel for these things, I return to your feeling of betrayal of the mother tongue as a sign of something more urgent in your approach, something words move towards—the place [Jack] Spicer takes us in his letter among letters to Lorca:

> Words are what sticks to the real. We use them to push the real, to drag the real into the poem. They are what we hold on with, nothing else. They are as valuable in themselves as rope with nothing to be tied to. I repeat—the perfect poem has an infinitely small vocabulary.
>
> Let me say: whatever it is about the choice

and arrangement of your words in translation (say, your translation of Horace), or whatever it is about how Horace politically harasses you in the original so that you desire to politically harass Horace back in translation; whatever it is about the choice and arrangement of any poet's words, they are sticking to something quite real. And, yes, they are dragging that reality into your translation and, as deeply, into your imagination of translation as disclosure. There is the urgency—there is the necessity: to disclose. To distance the close. To close the distance.

To act on the first—perhaps we need a different word than "betrayal." To act on the second—a different word than "reconciliation." Perhaps, to act on both at the same time, we need "a double-cross(ing)."

Meaning: you take your history, you take your place, you ask: "how do I (re)turn to what I have turned on?" That would be the risk, the double-cross,

> the double-crossing where the voices say: alternately
>
> You turn from the poem to translate.
>
> (Why—it could have been the poem you needed to write.)
>
>   Or:

You turn on the poem to translate.

(Why—it could have been the poem you needed to write.)

    And:

Your translation turns into the poem you turned on as if it were the poem you needed to write.

But it's not, not the poem.
Precisely.
It's always "as if."

It's never the poem (you needed to write?). Why? Simple—because it's the other one, the translation, the one outside your story, your language, your people, which had to be crossed,

As if—in the same way that Horace went over to the precedent Greek and came back like any translator bearing in his body language that which took him over from the outside. As if the translation was one way to get to the poem you needed to write but was a creation out of step with, out of difference with, out of defiance to your own home, story, language, people. At least for you.

For Horace, however, things are different. To be sure, and as I just read in an introduction to a book of his odes in English, "he thought of himself as a translator [with] a gift for turning Greek (I first wrote that "Greek" as "Freek") verse to Latin." But Horace was never out of step with his own Latin and his own Romans. If anything, his Greek models for his own poetry only enhanced his reputation as the rhythm of Rome. And his motives were other than yours, so that when he crossed over to the Greek and came back with "Greek verse" for his own Latin odes, he returned and was claimed an August(an) hero. So we're back to intention, the translator's intention when he crosses. How does one—and not just anyone, but a former esteemed Chancellor of The Academy of America Poets (poet Rosanna Warren)—cross into American English Horace's address to Caesar?

> don't
> let some quick breeze snatch you away from us
> in your scorn of our vices
>
> here, on earth, may you love great victories,
> here may you love us to call you Father and
>   Princeps,
> and don't let the Medes go on scot-free, raiding,
> while you lead us, Caesar.
>   ~Rosanna Warren

It's an American English which comes out of (t)his Latin:

> neve te nostris vitiis iniquum
> ocior aura
>
> tollat; hic magnos potius triumphos,
> hic ames dici pater atque princeps,

> neu sinas Medos equitare inultos,
> te duce, Caesar.

And then, of course, here you come, with your particularly sound mimicry of the emperor and the emperor's swooning flock, in the second Parade Ode, nailing the helium out of the spectacle floats:

> And never tell us our vice is iniquitous
> Or alter our ardor
>
> By talking. Here your major power can triumph.
> Here you'll love to be dictator, daddy and prince;
> Never sign us off as equals. Insult the
> Other! Caesar seize us!
>> ~Brandon Brown

I see here, Brandon, how you turn on Horace. I see how you nail him, how you spy on him, how you double-cross his praise of the leader and turn it into a mock commentary on the royal measure of things. As The Chancellor Poet's translation represents Horace's innocent adorned and adoring fans, yours makes them and their Caesar look, well, stupid and stupefied—or stupid because they're stupefied. It's brilliant. It's a gas. It's (a) laughing gas. It's moving, I mean: it's the right move you make to turn Horace inside out and disclose your grasp of the brilliance—and your comic disgust at the exercise—of formal power at work here. Yes, your Horace in English calls him on his intentions; yes, your Horace in English is not as safe or predictable or comfortable a read as the good former Chancellor poet's might be--isn't that why chancellors are chancellors, why their power is not your power or, as telling, why you are without their power, if that is what they are really with? But I wonder: as you're crossing Horace, what are you carrying across to "your own?" Granted, as a translator, you are spying on Horace, granted you are turning him over—thus, the common translator's expression, "he's turning over in his grave" (sic, my joke)—but I wonder: how do you make this practice useful for Americans, for your own? After all, you know this much is necessary to think through because you wrote about it in the preface to your translations of Horace:

> In this time, with the election by American citizens of a man who is the son of a leader, determined to both correct the shortcoming of his father and ensure the maintenance of a legacy of moral legislation, I found it difficult to translate Horace's unabashed praise of his leader, considering my own body's resistance to mine.

Brandon, I understand your difficulty in translating this kind of Horace in this time in America, and I understand the strategy to subvert his "unabashed" reverence. But for whom today, in this time in America, is he being undermined by you? Whose listening? What's your intention? What's more: if you claim that "a translator like any spy is at risk," what is it you really want to put at risk and leave without protection?

I ask the question because I think it has to do with why we are attracted to our subjects and what we want to discover and make vulnerable through their exposure. In "A Question of Accent," Murat Nemet-Nejat asks and brilliantly answers,

> Why did Kafka write *Amerika*, why was he attracted to the subject of the United States? German also accents Amerika. What did he hear in the word Oklahoma? A wild, alien, distant sound in German, Oklahoma! At the same time, an intimate sound, one of the rare words in English with vowel harmony, which is also, I imagine, in Czech. Kafka hears in Oklahoma the alien ground in which his private soul can nest itself, the synthesis between the powerful and the victim. That is why he associates his open-ended, endless nirvana of liberation in the Theater (Noah's Ark) of Oklahoma. What is the word Oklahoma after all, but the imprint of the Native American, the victim, the invaded in the language of the master, American English: the language

which embodies that peculiar combination, victim and victor possessing the same language, yoked together by fate.

Using American English as a poet is the outsider, the victim, embracing, emulating the language of the master, being constantly beset by the ambiguities of power.

To hear in a word something intimate and alien—what else is this but another way of "fertilizing one's Own through the mediation of what is foreign" or through what only appears to be foreign. It is to acknowledge as one's own and not one's own the appearance of the "alien ground in which (one's) private soul can nest itself." Or: it is to return home to disclose "the imprint of the invaded in the language of the master." Which means, in effect, to spy on "your own" as if you yourself were there to be revealed. Olson

> was right: people
> don't change. They only stand more
> revealed. I,
> likewise

And for you: whether as a translator or no translator, whether you think you're in Kansas (City) or you don't think you're in Kansas (City) anymore, the question is: how to turn to a history which is foreign and integral to yours and then use it once you return to "your own" so that you can "only stand more/revealed," to act the new basis for one's identity—the consciousness whose existence must be premised on one's existence in an other world?

Yours, Benjamin

REFERENCES

Benjamin, Walter. "The Task of the Translator" (1923). In Walter Benjamin, *Illuminations: Essays and Reflections*, ed. Hannah Arendt, trans. Harry Zohn. New York: Schocken Books, 1969.

Berman, Antoine. *The Experience of the Foreign: Culture and Translation in Romantic Germany*, trans. S. Heyvaert. Albany: State University of New York Press, 1992.

Brathwaite, Kamau. "History of the Voice." In Kamau Brathwaite, *Roots: Essays in Caribbean Literature*. Ann Arbor: University of Michigan Press, 1993.

"Brandon Brown and Benjamin Hollander." *Bombay Gin* 32 (2006): 176 ff.

Hindus, Milton, ed. *Charles Reznikoff: Man and Poet*. Orono, ME: National Poetry Foundation & The University of Main, 1984.

Hocquard, Emmanuel. *Blank Spots*, trans. Stacy Doris. *Un Bureau sur l'Atlantique: Le Gam #2*, 1997: http://epc.buffalo.edu/orgs/bureau/tb_a.html.

Hollander, Benjamin. In *A Review of Two Worlds: French and American Poetry in Translation*, ed. Béatrice Mousli. Los Angeles: Seismicity Editions, 2005.

Hollander, Benjamin. *Le livre de qui sont était : cinq sequences*. Grâne, France: Éditions Créaphis et Foundation Royamount pour la traduction française, 1997.

Hollander, Benjamin. *The Book of Who Are Was*. Los Angeles: Sun & Moon Press, 1997.

Hollander, Benjamin. "Ònòme." In Benjamin Hollander, *Vigilance*. Los Angeles: Beyond Baroque Books, 2005.

Hollander, Benjamin, *Ònòme*, trans. Emmanuel Hocquard, Vol. 4 of Format Américain. Buffalo, NY: Un Bureau sur l'Atlantique, 1994.

Horace, *Parade Odes*, trans. Brandon Brown.

Horace: The Odes, New Translations by Contemporary Poets, trans. Rosanna Warren, ed. J.D. McClatchy. Princeton, NJ: Princeton University Press, 2002.

Lerer, Yael. "The Word in Times of Crisis." *oznik.com*, November 16, 2004: http://oznik.com/words/041116.html.

Nemet-Nejat, Murat, "Questions of Accent." *ziyalan.com*: http://ziyalan.com/marmara/murat_nemet_nejat3.html. [Originally published in 1993 in *The Exquisite Corpse*.]

Olson, Charles. "Maximus, to Gloucester: Letter 2." In Charles Olson, *The Maximus Poems*, ed. George F. Butterick. Berkeley: University of California Press, 1985.

Raz-Krakotzkin, Amnon, cited in Lerer, "The World in Times of Crises" [see Lerer above].

Spicer, Jack. *After Lorca*. In *The Collected Books of Jack Spicer*, ed. Robin Blaser. Santa Rosa, CA: Black Sparrow Press, 1975.

W. dreams, like Phaedrus, of an army of thinker-friends, thinker-lovers. He dreams of a thought-army, a thought-pack, which would storm the philosophical Houses of Parliament. He dreams of Tartars from the philosophical steppes, of thought-barbarians, thought-outsiders. What distances would shine in their eyes!

~Lars Iyer

www.babelworkinggroup.org

www.ingramcontent.com/pod-product-compliance
Lightning Source LLC
Chambersburg PA
CBHW070849160426
43192CB00012B/2376